"The poems in Sal Marici's collection, *Sneezing Coyotes*, are full of color and scent, critters and questions of faith and spiritual seeking. Also casseroles and cattle, familiar and faraway landscapes. They will take you into and beyond what you already know. You'll want to read and reread these poems for the many ways they make 'emptiness a welcome place.'"
—Rebecca Wee, author of *Uncertain Grace*

I0799890

SNEEZING COYOTES

Salvatore
Marici

Ice Cube Press, LLC, (Est. 1991)
North Liberty, Iowa, USA

Sneezing Coyotes

First Edition
ISBN 9781948509312

Ice Cube Press, LLC (Est. 1991)
1180 Hauer Drive
North Liberty, Iowa 52317 USA
www.icecubepress.com | steve@icecubepress.com

The paper used in this publication meets the minimum requirements of the American National Standard for Information Sciences—Permanence of Paper for Printed Library Materials, ANSI Z39.48-1992.

Cover art: Kathy Negaard
Drawing of author: Edward Schiffer

Previously Published:
-*Poetry Quarterly*: Selective Killings Before Winter, The Falling Self, Disturbed Circadian Rhythm
-*Toasted Cheese*: Vagina Bowl Workshop
-*Three Line Poetry*: On the Boardwalk in Corkscrew Swamp Sanctuary
-*Cacti Fur*: As We Wait for His Transport to Cremation
-*Brief Wilderness*: Goodbye to an Unfilled Want.
-2017 Blog for Collins Poetry Residency (Midwest Writing Center): Look for a Sign, Any Sign
-Midwest Writing Center Press: *These Interesting Times*: Surviving 2020 in the Quad Cities Midwest Writing Center, A Covid 19 Halloween in Rural Western IL: MWC Survival Anthology
-*Writers Block* e-magazine: When We Had a Torn Net Before We Met also placed 2nd in Iron Pen Contest and Dancing poetry Festival
-*Aromatica Poetica*: Sneezing Coyotes, Gringo Meets Guatemala's Pigs Easter Meal from Scratch, Acquire Self Esteem from Fats
-2020 Wormfarm Institutes's Fermentation Festival Guide: Changing Landscapes

For a heart stained in anger grows weak and grows bitter.
You become your own prisoner as you watch yourself sit there
Wrapped up in a trap of your very own
Chain of sorrow.
—John Prine

If you build up the soil with organic material,
the plants will do just fine.
—John Harrison

Table of Contents

Zoonotic Spillover 7
Man in Tropical Shirts Writes Poetry 8
On the Boardwalk in Corkscrew Swamp Sanctuary 10
As We Wait for His Transport to Cremation 11
Safe Place 12
Sneezing Coyotes 13
Look For a Sign, Any Sign 14
Roaming Souls Who Did Not Have a Passage Ritual 15
Survivor Prays for Victims while Christ Gets Whip 16
Cut Supply Routes 17
A Potter's House Along the Mekong River in Cambodia 18
Facets of Cambodia's Rats 20
An Afternoon in Sticky Hanoi 21
Capitalism 22
To Survive Walk Straight 23
Disturbed Circadian Rhythm 24
Re-Caught Inside the Rush to Get There 25
A Crow Claws an Overreaching Branch 26
Wasted Carbon Foot Prints 27
Chicago's Loop Food Chain 28
Creative Marketing 29
Transport 30
Gringo Meets Guatemala's Pig Easter Meal from Scratch 31
Gringo Meets Guatemala's Pig Pigs with Homes 32
Gringo Meets Guatemala's Pig Assimilate into the Culture 33
Need a "2" to Become a Peace Corps Volunteer 34
Don't Tread Beneath Me 35
Sinusitis 36
Guatemala's Women 37
Vagina Bowl Making Workshop 38
Anxiety of Leaving You...... 39
Goodbye to an Unfilled Want 40
Bewitching a Six-Year-Old 41
Mom's Meal 42
Poems in Casseroles 43

Sneaks Out of Oven 44
September Visual on the Root River Bike Path 45
A Cyclist's Astral Body Ecstasy 46
Haiku - Mount the Unicorn 47
Acquire Self Esteem from Fats 48
Compulsive Behavior of a Brainedwashed Man 49
Became Father McKenzie 50
Used Put Aside 51
Salutations 52
The Falling Self 53
Desertification 54
Tales From a Non-Savior 55
Caskets in Demand 56
Irma Kills Creation in Puerto Rico 57
Selective Killings Before Winter 58
Monocultures...... 59
Bring the Spring Tilth Inside 60
Changed Landscape 61
Lineage 62
When We Had a Torn Net Before We Met 64
A Life Awareness 65
A Covid-19 Halloween in Rural Western IL 66
Larry 68
1960's Barber Shop in Chicago's Northwest Side 69
From Play to Write 70
Particles at the Edge of Life 71
Credits 72
About the author 73

Zoonotic Spillover

The coronavirus pandemic is one of "nature's responses" to humans ignoring the current ecological crisis. – Pope Francis

Bites,
feces monkeys' flick,
breathe butchered meat.
Infectious agents jump species.
Codes mutate billion times over
until a protein sequence fools to
manufacture. New agents attack,
attach, blow holes in membranes
of adjacent cells, penetrate
freaks hosts' immune systems
triggers destruction of beings
like the people chased from shorelines.
Rising water floods their homes
forces them to move
where rivers, oceans won't reach.
Refugees make settlements
crowded without running water
where viruses live in bats,
monkeys, plants, anything alive.

Man in Tropical Shirts Writes Poetry

I would believe in God but no one can prove it. - George Mathon

George
wears silk shirts.
Tailor cut.
Birds, flowers align in the front
when buttons fasten holes.

He settles in his canvas chair
on piers where
mangrove roots build islands,
sawgrass saws wind
egrets wade.

Inside a blue notebook
ink scripts his thoughts
sentences about ecosystems
cultural-biodiversity, us, him.

For sixteen years
his missing and fused vertebrae
induce stiffness.
He can't swivel,
                    bend,
                            plant seeds,
                            pick eggplant.

Fluid fills his one lung
over inflates if he scuba dives.
Unwanted tissue grows
turns into hard lumps,
hurts beyond aches.

He slows his body.
He leans into a couch
lays laptop on his lap
taps keys, revises.

Poems become
his eternity.

On the Boardwalk in Corkscrew Swamp Sanctuary

An Alligator's jaw chops
a turtle's shell. The crack breaks
silent air at Lettuce Lake. We stop.

As We Wait for His Transport to Cremation

Dedicated to George Mathon

George's body lies in bed
mouth ajar. His skin
each minute turns
in a shade of white
paler than before.

In front of his grandpa's corpse
grandson flips through tropical shirts.
The few items George's daughter
did not pack for me
to take to Goodwill.

Grandson picks one. He pulls
his t-shirt over his head.
Slips his arms through sleeves.
When buttons fasten holes
birds, flowers align.

A friend of George
who has the same name
who influenced George's poetry
wears a tropical shirt he selected
from the stack.

George would smile
if he could see them
wear him.
But he said no afterlife exists.

Safe Place

Dedicated to Ryan Capriotti

Blankets keep his body warm
as no blood pumps through
veins. Pillow cushions his head.
His smile radiates.
Ear buds plays classical piano.
Chords lift his spirit
through the window.

Sneezing Coyotes

Day before the vet injects
barbiturates on top of Valium,

damp autumn dusk
settles in the prairie behind my house.
Whiskey burns my belly.
I dig her grave thigh deep.

Tonight, the moon's surface reflects the sun,
spreads silvery light over native plants,
Coyotes sniff the hole's fresh-turned soil.

Today, the last heat this black cat will generate,
leaves, passes through her cardboard coffin
warms my lap. Ruby curls as if
asleep in her basket on the windowsill

except wrapped
in the minor league baseball t-shirt
my brother bought me.
Kathy and I blanketed her with the slip
Ruby slept on when it held her pillow
cushioned against mine.

I lie on my stomach at the hole's edge.
Box wedges against walls.
Shovel chisels one side, five inches.
Carton slides - bottoms.
Kathy shakes a black pepper tin.
Grinds fall on the thick paper.
Every six scoops of earth
she scatters more powder
till the last shake
dusts the last layer of soil.

Look For a Sign, Any Sign

With the priest's siblings in the pews
he sprinkles holy water, sways a censor,
smoke dusts his mother's casket.
Cancer killed her at 67.

Two days before,
ceiling lights flicker
over a table of candles
in red jars. Some lit.
Heat waves over the glow
like exposed coals in a campfire.
One of her other sons
the mailman wipes
salty water his eyes drip
then lower the lids.

Few minutes pass,
he opens them,
sees one wick
he thought unlit burns
in this empty hall
with closed windows
no running fans.

This flame wiggles circles
bright clear a graceful dance
like planchettes glide answers
on Ouija boards.

Roaming Souls Who Did Not Have a Passage Ritual

A cement wall with crumbled segments
surrounds this Buddhist Complex.
Inside a pagoda stands
whitewashed one-story rectangle
with worn-ornate roof.
One of the few Khmer Rouge
did not destroy. It held prisoners.

Today inside this religious complex
on bare soil in the shade of trees
villagers lay their dead
on three pipes anchored into
two rows of paralleled charred bricks,
stacked thigh-high.

Outside these grounds
farmers unearth bones, rotten cloth
relics from those the regime killed.
Inside lingering ghosts
suck the livings' energy
cry at cremations.

Survivor Prays for Victims while Christ Gets Whip

The Dirty Wars were a series of bloody dictatorships that repressed the civilian population during the 70s and 80s in Latin America. The people will never recover completely. – Southfront

In Chicago's Saint Michael Cathedral
as he does every Friday a Latino about 70
stands before the altar on the polished marble floor.
He bends, grabs a poster in a pile to his right
lifts, holds black & white images
of young adult faces. Abductees, males,
females, military juntas' victims
whose genitals cattle prods zapped.
Heads bullets shot through.
Bodies dumped into mass graves.
People tossed alive from helicopters
onto water hard as stone.
Each photograph covers
the griever's neck to thighs,
extends beyond his body's width.
He focuses his and the gone eyes
on the tabernacle
prays in monotone voice.

Tourists in the aisles whisper,
study stain glass the sun illuminates
sprays them the story of Jesus
when on his knee, his shoulder bears a cross
piercing thorns crown his head
under blue skies
white clouds patch.

Cathedral's vastness muffles pleas
the survivor recites in Spanish.
He places the disappeared to his left
twists his torso keeps his eyes wide
glances at empty pews.

Cut Supply Routes

I hold a hatchet arm raises
blade strikes trees around trunks
bark peels like paint
exposes bands of white moist wood
breaks sugar transports
from food-making leaves
to where needed. I cause
deaths from starvation.

A Potter's House Along the Mekong River in Cambodia

Her husband pushes a shovel
into the mountain' side, scoops clay,
carries it home on his back.
Wife grabs five handfuls.
She becomes a pottery wheel, walks around
and around, slaps bulges, splashes water,
curves slippery surface into a vase.

I ask the guide what the potter thinks
as she spins around the vase. He interprets,
Thankful my husband quit drinking palm wine.
Will we have food tomorrow?

The side of the dirt street where shade comforts
a cane supports the village's elder slanted back.
She looks skinny but weighs more than
when she slaved in the paddies
dawn to night under the Khmer Rouge
who decided because she could not read,
because she had calloused hands,
they would not stab a bamboo spear
through her skull. Because of luck,
diseases did not rot her in a field.

She, the only town's senior shuffles
to the metal roofed shelter where
fourteen American tourists sit on a log,
its length split in half, chunks of wood
prop the seat to a bench height.
Despite the Potter's verbal don't
this deaf woman's hand sweeps
ceramic trinkets displayed for sale
on a table to its middle. She sits.

Potter says, "*Old lady comes.*
Malnutrition did not kill her
when Pol Pot allocated
¼ cup of rice water twice per day.
We feed her, so do neighbors."

Facets of Cambodia's Rats

Rat breeders gather
To primp and parade their best
—Thomas Lux

A black rat waits in a doorway.
Its black eyes wide, nose twitches,
sniffs the wet market's
fear the living creatures for sale emit,
blood & flesh.
It scurries pass a display

of rats skinned, gutted,
cracked at the ribs, spread.
Good country rats, healthy rats, rice rats,
rats who eat whole grains, not garbage.
Monsoons chase them to higher grounds
farmers catch, sell, save their rice crops.

Through the rural regions
brown rats bred in Tanzania
wear harnesses hooked to overhead cables
guide their two feet plus bodies
through fields landmines remain.
Twitching noses scent TNT.
Their 2.6 lbs. do not detonate.

After a day of detecting explosives,
Magawa walks her college shoulders
nibbles peanuts, bananas,
sometimes watermelon rinds.
She keeps farmers' and children limbs attached
not blown from the devices Americans' left.
A medal hangs around her neck.

An Afternoon in Sticky Hanoi

The metallic grinds of scooter's gears
blend into sizzles of salty sauce
frying chicken, fish, pork, vegetables
in woks, metal spoons clang
on sidewalks in front of homes
where customers sit on beer crates,
eat next to women whose small feet
soak in pans of water
while they get their fingernails trimmed.

At an intersection, a man sits on a curb,
eyes closed; thumbs touch middle fingers.
Centimeters from his sandaled toes
scooter tires roll. Pedestrians' legs
brush the meditating man's knees
another sense from streets he knows
passes through his flowing mind,
exits into the universe.

Capitalism Along the Mekong River, Cambodia

Road Scholar seniors sit on their butts
in ox carts, two per wagon
rolling along a dirt road.
Two scooters pass us.
Children of 8 - 10 years
run alongside. Outstretched hands
offer small flowers
they picked on roadsides,
drawings of butterflies in blue ink
on sheets ripped from notebooks.
Tourists instructed not to buy,
teach them no future in handouts
give them reason to stay in school
take notes, learn the three Rs.

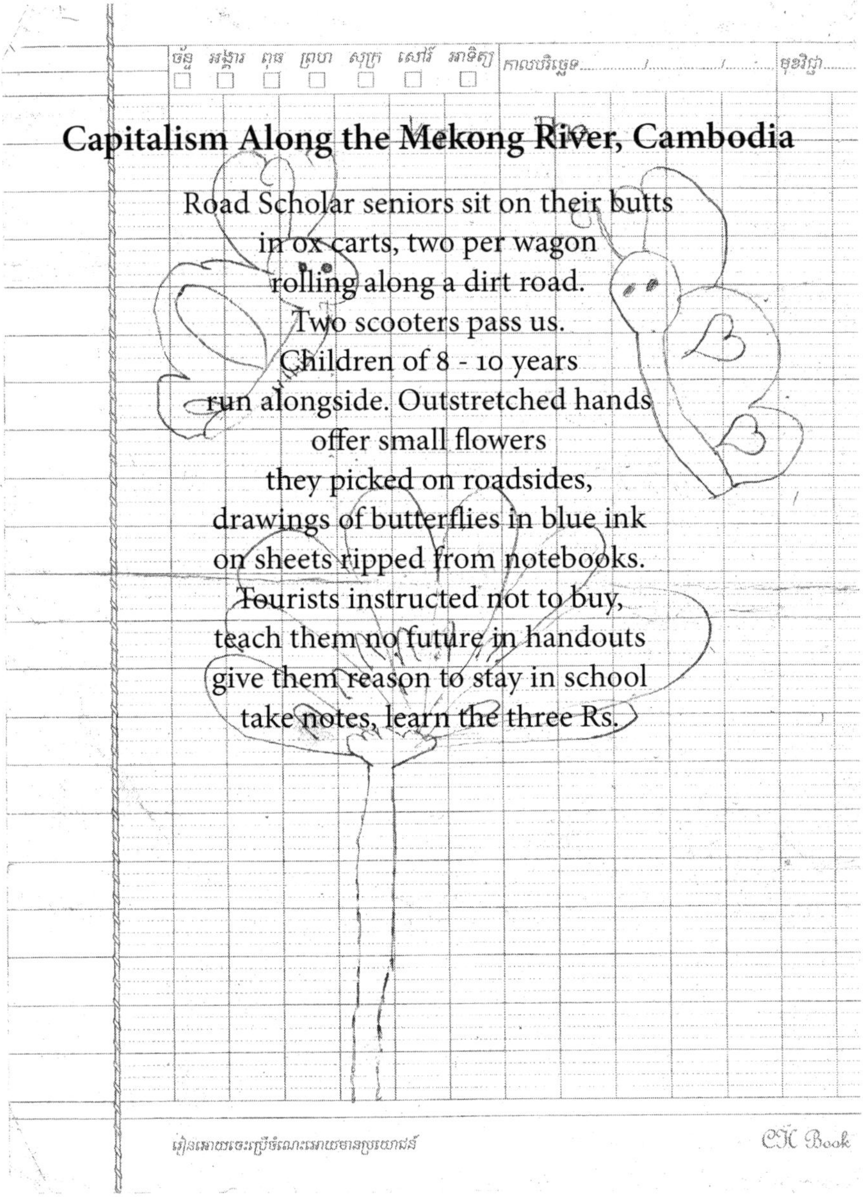

drawing by Kim Tha

To Survive Walk Straight

A township road in the Midwest
cuts through corn fields, orchards.
On gravel pressed into tar
a squirrel's eyes swell black.
He stops, stands on two legs
head whips left to right.
Impulse drops him on all fours,
about-face runs.
Pickup's tire meets the rodent
before he reaches the ditch.

In Hanoi I stand on a curb.
My head turns right, left.
detect a 10 second window,
decide,
step into the street.
Adrenaline bulges my eyes.
I blaze a steady pace on a linear path.

Scooters & few cars
twist & swirl around
predictions of my actual locations
resemblance of Mississippi steamboat pilots
navigate appearing rocks in rapids.

Disturbed Circadian Rhythm

Our plane leaves the ground 10 p.m. in Taiwan.
Bodies squash between seats' arms,
cruise at 500 mph, travel thirteen hours.
One a.m. in San Francisco,
my head swirls clockwise. Hotel bed whirls counter.
If I hold a globe
I don't know if I should spin the world left or right
can't decipher if we traveled east to west or west to east,
if we arrived the night before or the night after.

Re-Caught Inside the Rush to Get There

On the ramp's shoulder
to Delray Beach,
an ambulance passes cars.
A man late for the beach
follows in his white sedan blocks the firetruck.
Flashing lights beam over the jam.
The four-lanes revolves its tires
twice every three minutes.

Last year in January,
cream sooths coffee's bitter edge
Retried I sit in my kitchen chair.
Stare outside into rural IL.
Ice films two-lane road,
flat slide to the town's offices.
A driver accelerates,
crosses solid line to pass.
Oncoming pickup appears at the bend.

Thirty minutes later in Southeast Florida
I see two cars crumpled to their front seats.
One landed between the interstate and exit lane.
The other sits in the way. Ambulance pries the
stalled traffic, gets to someone who has no shirt.
Sun absorbed pavement burns his back.

The woman who examined the injured
scurries between vehicles to her white sedan
parked on the shoulder. Same looking car
as the guy who drove on the narrow edge
a half-hour ago. Her face pleads to merge.
I like others shake my head no.

A Crow Claws an Overreaching Branch

Beak open, stretch, I see red
inside her mouth. Rapid caws spew.
The Miccosukee Indian asks,
What do you want big boy?
Repeats the question
with each bird's plea.

Rest of the protesters sit
on the ground a foot from
serrated ferns
interlocked under trees.

With sweat on our skin,
we trek US 41
five days in the Everglades.
Our plea to stop the laying
of bike paths, parking lots,
construction of quick shops,
concrete, asphalt
rain can't penetrate

not like dirt lanes off the highway.
Tire ruts lead trucks to sites
oil companies drill.
Frack if they could
on nine-acre concrete pads.

Wasted Carbon Foot Prints

In Naples Florida
on a Monday winter afternoon
boomers scramble for scarce stools
driven by half price drinks & appetizers
at a restaurant with outdoor sitting.
A blonde woman fresh from a salon
flaunts her pageboy haircut,
nabs one.

She bites,
crunches pungent spice.
Her long red nails clasp
the stem of a martini glass.
She tells the bartender to take back
the plate of thin slice tuna steak
        fishing boat caught, vacuumed in plastic
sushi grade raw inside
        refrigerated truck delivered
seared with black peppercorns
        spice shipped from India
some embedded in flesh
she could have scraped with a fork.

Chicago's Loop Food Chain

A spatula could scoop
the rats' squashed bald tail,
flesh, organs covered with
skin dried as a hide
spotted with sparse brown hair
on Adams Street at Michigan Ave.,
in an area rent costs four grand
to sleep, cook, watch TV in
high rises' studios.
Below on the sidewalks
people sleep on cardboard
hope someone drops a dollar
on their claimed domain.
We walk the streets.
Rats watch us through sewer grates
behind trash bins in alleys
where restaurants throw scraps
diners left on their plates
homeless compete for.

Creative Marketing

Producers feed cattle corn
enriched with antibiotics, hormones.
Clear wrap seals foam trays,
traps pumped carbon monoxide
makes Rib Eye blood red.
Carnivores at meat counters seek flesh
butchered from animals
raised in stalls, no space to turn.
Checkout we pay $14.95 per pound to eat
flaccid muscles marbled with fat
what we hope our bodies will not become.

Transport

Farmers' switches make Iowa pigs
walk ramps. Each adds density
inside trailers. Those who can
stick snouts in slits of metal walls.

Jews forced to climb into freight cars
press against wood walls
inhaled air leaked through cracks.

All howl their fears
their wants for water.

Gringo Meets Guatemala's Pigs Easter Meal from Scratch

Guatemalans slice pigs' jugulars.
Adobe walls throughout villages
absorb squeals. Those alive
watch the hanging bleed.

Mothers with daughters wrap
banana leaves around ground corn
moisten to an almost mush,
drop a dab of boiled pork.
Pots steam tamales over wood fires.

Deep in the masa I find
a jagged piece of pig's skin
tough as an elephant hide
with one black curly hair.

Gringo Meets Guatemala's Pigs
Pigs with Homes

Every morning wives swing brooms
smack pigs' black butts
chase them out of adobe houses
into Guatemala's rural roads.
Red dust ankle deep.
Slick when wet.

Triangles made from scrap wood
clasp pigs' necks. Stops snouts
from rooting fields. Front legs bump
bottom slabs, nudge them into a two-step.

Dusk, they dance over their thresholds.

Gringo Meets Guatemala's Pigs Assimilated into the Culture

As I speak to the Guatemalan sandal maker…

He carves tires to fit feet.
Inside the adobe house,
his wife smacks pig's black butt.
Swine trots front doorstep where I sit,
brushes my leg.

… my sentence does not pause.

Need a "2" to Become a Peace Corps Volunteer

One bulb hangs from a beam
under a tin roof adobe walls support.
Light shines on me & two-woman examiners.
We sit in wooden chairs. One asks in Spanish,
Is it all right the mattress has flees?
I say *Sì*. They score me 1 plus.

The county director says *you tried*
you get second chance.

Sunday, I drink rum from pint bottles
during a drill with a Spanish instructor,
a Guatemalan, in his house.
We talk about family photos,
dead people with blank stares
nailed on pink-painted mud walls.
Dirt streaks, cobwebs in corners.
You will pass tomorrow, he assures.

On a purple bus to the Capital
spit aids the swallow of a pink pill,
10-mg-Valium. Head rises to ether.
I speak many subjects, ask questions,
give answers in wrong tense, gender
while gestures guide my hands.
Score 2 minus, enough to pass.

Don't Tread Beneath Me

Like the loudening whirls
1950's sci-fi movies emit
when flying saucers land,
the eeriness
in howler monkeys' roars
crescendo till it whelms
Guatemala's rainforest.
They nest in trees,
pick shit from their asses
flick on intruders.
Piss splashes gringos' hats.
Tourists in Tikal tilt their heads,
click cameras, say *awesome*.

Back home
humidity stuffs my Florida condo,
treehouse high. People in parking lot
see tropical plastic plants
against lanai's grey screen.

A delivery truck arrives.
Its diesel engine rattles repress,
its fumes choke the muse,
overcomes the poem
my mind began to compose.
Two men open – slam doors.
A rolling rumble
raises truck's back shutter.
Lift hums couch to ground.

I a naked primate sit unshaven
with my back to them so I can view
pine and palm trees, my jungle.
I grunt, fart but don't pick my butt.

Sinusitis

Passageways hidden
like those in Mayan temples
lead to tombs; warm-moist

caves under my face
where mucus flourishes.
Florescent green filaments
sway like coral
before oceans warmed.

Drifting pollen
a black pepper itch
inside my nose.
Nerves trigger brain.
Sneeze with hope after a blow
yellow goop plops in tissue.
Nothing ejects.

Guatemala's Women

Plastic stems punched
into flimsy flipflops
slip between
big & second toes.

Bundles of firewood,
water in plastic jugs
balance on heads.
Neck veins bulge.

Life's weight
toils each step
flattens calloused feet.

Vagina Bowl Making Workshop

Photos of Tigerlily's vagina guide
women's fingers press,
curve beige clay,
cast intentions to the earth
cuddle in their hands.
Bear babies if want.
Lubricate after menopause.

Like priests with chalices
I raise arms
hold vessels of life.
Hail to vaginas' miracles,
women's marvels.
Tilt, drink.

Anxiety of Leaving You

With your back against the door
your green eyes sprinkle sparkles
like a fairy waving her wand.
You barefooted in red sweats
toes bent on top of left foot.
I reach for the doorknob.
You step, let me pass.
I do not sweep
scattered fondness
off my coat and cap.

Goodbye to an Unfilled Want

It seems Lin emerged from the fairy woods
where tree line meets grass. The site
she pitched her tent for twenty years
at this pagan festival.
Kathy and I creep the van
packed with wet camp gear
along the one lane dirt road
between the field and labyrinth.

This morning the sky wants to turn blue
so sunrays can color misty bands
into rainbows. Yet a sunlight like shine
highlights Lin's skyclad body.
Her skin glistens lingering wetness
the slickness on her buttocks, legs, heels.
Silver hair stops at the arousal spot
on her lower back
bent over a collapsed tent. Her fingers
nudge a pole through fabric,
push it out of its sleeve.

Like oceans under full moon
Lin pulls me. I shift in park,
tell Kathy *I need to say goodbye*.

Bewitching a Six-Year-Old

Jane whines, spits
cayenne pepper flakes
mixed with salt crystals,
dried tomatoes. A rub
her father composed,
spread on ribs, smoked.

Mother clears table.
Serves cake
she baked from scratch.
Spongy layers of chocolate
tuckpointed like a bricked wall
with vanilla pudding.
Swirls of butter cream speckle.

Jane's blue eyes widen,
forehead wrinkles
same seriousness
working poor decide
which bill to pay.

Dessert sweetens Jane's taste buds.
Sugary stimulus commands her brain to
forget the burning of
her last spellbinding complaint.

Mom's Meal

Knotted knuckles limit her grip
on the fork she uses to prod
the yellowed bubble of a poached egg.
It shakes. Third poke breaks
its membrane. Yoke spills
over the clotted white protein
she cuts
nibbles twice
then pushes the plate.
Buttered cinnamon toast
stays untouched.

Poems in Casseroles

Poet savors a collective taste
masterful chef creates.
Intuition, craft, select spices.
Knows if dish needs
two or three pinches or handfuls.
Makes tuna casserole something
you order in restaurants.

Sneaks Out of Oven

Inside pumpkin pie mixture
heat arouses oils in cinnamon
                    cloves nutmeg ginger vanilla
        lifts excited droplets,
        swirls them in enclosed chamber
collective scent whiffs
vapors of sugars
                            caramelized in baking apples
                            on the bottom rack
blesses aroma's glow
with a sweet coating
hovers autumn's oranges & reds.

September Visual on the Root River Bike Path

When sunlight shines spaces between walnut leaves
streams of gold splinters filter through canopies.
Those my solar shield catches curve
around its curved plastic. One
sliver follows another
like snow in a
headlight
beam.

A Cyclist's Astral Body Ecstasy

Steady wind pushes his back
aids his legs spin pedals
rotating chain engage sprockets.
Pumped tires revolve
whoosh around curves
an inch above asphalt.

Haiku

mount the unicorn
fly into your unconscious
seal cracks traumas made

Acquire Self Esteem from Fats

Kathy says to me
Wish you would have more self-confidence
as we eat baked tuna and egg noodles
mixed with green peas
chicken broth glistens
cheddar covers.
I reply *me too.*

Her fingers peel melted cheese
from her plate. Fork pierces
brown bubbled curd.
She flicks it on mine
because dairy has fat.

I want grease. It lubricates.
Slides life's rejections.
Makes emptiness a welcome place
discoveries slip into.

Compulsive Behavior of a Brainwashed Man

I see turbulent flames pulsate
through the roof of my house
while I ride my bike
ten miles from home
because I can't remember
if I left the stove on
though I am sure
after I fried my egg
I turned the burner knob to off.

The show "It Will Go Wrong"
streams in my head.
At the end of an episode
a rerun or a new one
with a different plot
same theme plays.
Continuous airings wear me
like a spot of constant friction
of a baggy sock against a heel
bloats into a blister.

Became Father McKenzie

Father McKenzie, writing the words of a sermon
that no one will hear—Lennon/McCartney

The phone's speaker, set loud
projects a repeating electronic
Da-a Loop – Da-a-Loop – Da-a-Loop
A swipe on the red to decline
green to answer
or let the noise stop on its own.
How or if my finger moves
depends if I have
the guts – the energy
to speak to a human
something I don't do every day.
Became comfortable not to.
While I write poems, no one reads.

Used, Put Aside

Lead from artists' pencils
elevates and thickens thighs
turning the nude's contour
in black on oatmeal paper.
Faint rubbing sounds
circulates the studio where
I pose on a platform.
My rigid muscles beg massaging.
itching skin unscratched
for three hours.

Artists pack pencils in pouches,
insert sketches in portfolios

who unpack at home,
open photos on phones
they took of me.
When drawings feel finished
I lie in piles of nudes and portraits,
of forgotten drawings.

Salutations

(for Dan Kluto)

When we meet,
I raise the middle finger on my right-hand,
arm rotates like a pitcher warming up until
my left-hand catches, slaps at the elbow bend
five times, all at you my sleazy friend
while I shout a loud and pointed
FUCK YOU ASSHOLE.
This ritual pierces pressure
like popping balloons inside my head.
Regardless where I give you this greeting
in your house, public beer garden
it rids half of my stress
coffee stout drowns the rest.

The Falling Self

My identity's roots deepen as I talk,
maybe laugh at least smile to people
at Unity Church/ condo lobby/ market /
after a reading / teaching a workshop /
during weekly beer meets yet
my esteem leaks like a faucet
with a worn rubber washer
drips till it slips like rocks on
slicked mud gravity pulls in thunderstorms
eroded like a mountainside after an avalanche.

Desertification

When the sky drops rain on this tropical mountain denuded of trees, I level my eyes to its slope. See dark soil mix with rainwater. Chocolate drinks run off. During dry season, each year more days added, winds pickup grit - - spray like buckshot. Hard minerals from dime size to stones used to build fences appear. Pebbles bruise my calloused feet. Under the sun in fields of red dust ankle high, I make space for seeds. Lift rocks. Carry them aside. Heat they hold burns my hands.

before hopeful rains
peasants sow inside dry winds
water moves soil - seeds

Tales from a Non-Savior

Salvador, *Salva la selva!*
the shaman tells me.
We drink moonshine
mixed with water and lime
heated over a fire
in an Amazon tributary.
He assigns me a mission,
gives me the title
the Jungle's Savior
save from oil companies,
people who wear shoes.

I hire Guatemalan boys
pay with
black beans, rice, corn oil.
We fill black bags with soil,
poke holes, drop tree seeds.
Water them in the nursery
during the dry season.
Rains come we give to people to
plant seedlings in their fields
on the slopes of Volcán Suchitán.
Landslides lift roots,
droughts dehydrate,
machetes cut stems
thick as twigs.
Fuel to cook black beans.

Caskets in Demand

In a denuded rainforest
campesinos' wives
walk nine kilometers in dust,
ankle high on a dirt road.
It stops at a river where
women scoop water.
Five-gallon containers
balance on their heads.

No wood to gather, fuel to boil.
Amoebas, giardia
live in droplets on wet plates.
Ingested: stomachs cramp, gurgle.
Nutrients suspended in water
run through intestines.
Kill infants, old, weak.

Irma Kills Creation in Puerto Rico

Before and after Irma's eye abrupt stillness,
sustained winds lift leaves, yank roots.
Rain saturates pores in fertile grounds.
Slurries of organic matter
slide on mountain's slopes
puddle in flats of valleys.
Muck covers
insects' landing pads,
petals brushed with colors
brighter than rainbows.
Flowers' fragrances smothered.

Bees buzz for pollen.

Selective Killings Before Winter

The brush hog's blades spin,
sever tall ragweed, grasses,
morning glory vines, cone flowers.
The rolling mower lays mats of
chopped plants. Green pigments
stain my sneakers. I hold a hatchet
before the autumn's leafless trees,
most a few years older than saplings.
Steel strikes a circle
around these young trees.
Cut bark peels like paint
expose bands of slippery wood.
Break sugar transports
from food-making leaves
to where needed.

After winter,
no new twigs sprout
on these posts where
song birds peck burrowing insects
fly into bare crowns
sing above
networks of living systems
grown from the dead in soil.

Monocultures

Richness whiffs into the air
when disk break ground,

earthworms squinch under sun
squiggle retreat into black spongy soil

built from the dead
microorganisms, worms digest

stubble from last year's harvest,
animals who died of prey, illnesses

not from poisons farmers
sprayed on corn, soybeans

injected into earth to terminate
aphids, rust, nematodes, weeds, etcetera

same pesticides kill nontargeted individuals
of various species who give and take

what their ecosystems demand
to keep their homes in balance.

Bring the Spring Tilth Inside

Loam I cultivate in my garden
beds in my toe prints
fills creases around heels.

Powder like graphite
coats my soles. Lubricated,
I slide on laminated floors
throughout the house.

Windows open.
Breeze touches.
Ceiling fans lift sweat
from my skin, blow it
through screens.

With my soil, I
lay on crisp sheet.
Its corner pockets
clasp memory foam.
I sink then float
few feet above earth.

Changed Landscape

Rain falls
through cracks in a roof
of a barn built in early 1900's.
Melted snow seeps,
into gray-splintered boards
once painted red
when horses, cows, and pigs
lived on an 80-acre farm
the farmer's great grandkids sold.

Lineage

Lure to Aachen Germany

Fountain in the city's center pours
thermal water. We put our hands
in the flow, feel the comfort as
when conquerors soak their muscles.
Healing powers entice to build houses,
establish trade, governments, societies.

To Walk in Comfort on History

After the Neanderthals:
Celts, Germanic tribes, Romans,
Middle Age chancellors, emperors, Hitler
and today natives with DNA remnants
blended with middle east arrivals
smother settlements, cities,
build over burial sites, altars, garbage pits.
Take stones from walls to reuse.
Clear bombed buildings. Construct.

I buy foot pads in Aachen Germany
at a pharmacy with three windows
built into the floor
showcase Roman structures
below our feet.

Bathing in Aachen Germany

We get naked in a co-ed changing room
stay bare, the rule, to go upstairs
have steam sweat dirt
from pores in herbal air
bathe in same water
that ran in aqueducts into baths
under domes Romans built.
Reminiscent of what I see
on my back floating.

When We Had a Torn Net Before We Met

each of us cuts twine
severed from adjacent rectangles.
Each scissors a cord wrapped around a spool,
flips it over, under,
flies it through a loop,
pulls into reattaching knots.

Since our encounter,
you & I scalpel frailness
from our nets,
keep used but wanted patches
like worn slippers.
With surgeon's precision
we stitch old sections
to the new we weave
in presence of the other.

Our flesh fills open spaces
we share on this new
queen size hammock.
We don't fear of falling
through rips.

A Life Awareness

I carry the
Sgt. Peppers' Lonely Hearts Club Band Album
to the kitchen table.
Dad reads *Chicago Tribune*.
He folds it. I point to people on the cover
I watched on black & white TV
Mae West, WC Fields,
Humphrey Bogart, Marilyn Monroe,
Marlon Brando, pre-1967 Beatles.
We study faces,
cartoon likeness on cardboard,
to see who Dad knows.
I ask, *What is a lonely-hearts club?*
He explains, *it's what people join*
who want to meet someone special.

Oh, the eleven-year-old boy says about loneliness.

A COVID-19 Halloween in Rural Western IL

In the year of the dead,
believers mask mouths and noses

while non-believers send
Dr. Fauci death threats.

My neighbor follows his warnings,
don't take their kids into Port Byron

let them shout "trick or treat"
to anybody who opens a door

five miles as the crow flies
in a town without stoplights

from the cornfields butted
against the four-house cluster.

A princess and Wonder Woman
ring my door bell, giggle "treat."

Wonder Woman stretches her arm,
hands me a paper lunch bag.

Homemade chocolate cookies,
couple Snickers bite size bars,

corn chips and a can of craft beer
their dad added

on the eve of the Day of the Dead.
The day the thin veil rises

between the dead and the living
in a year the line gets blurrier

multiple passings pass as
believers survive
in isolation.

Larry

Thank you, Larry, for Facebooking me.
At age seven, we bought a box mix, griddled pancakes.
Around the time I punched you in the nose till it bled.
I bossed you but you stayed friends with me.

At age seven we bought a box mix, griddled pancakes.
We scrambled eggs but never baked.
I bossed you but you stayed friends with me.
We garbage picked, found Playboys, gawked under trees.

As kids we scrambled eggs, yet we never baked.
You became a chef, mastered world's cuisines, seared steaks.
Many years before, we garbage picked, found Playboys, gawked.
You quit being a chef because you wanted family time.

You became a chef, mastered world cuisines, seared steaks,
before you bought an air & heat shop, before you had spare time.
You quit the chef gig because you wanted to be with family.
Now you keep people comfortable, without ripping them off.

You bought an air & heat shop, started volunteering.
Communities prized your citizen, business awards.
Now you keep customers comfortable, without ripping them off.
Grateful people want to shake your hand.

Communities prized your citizen and business awards.
If we meet, will you punch my nose, make it bleed?
Will you want to shake my hand?
We have not seen each other for fifty years.

If we meet, will you punch my nose?
When we were seven, I punched yours till it bled.
We have not seen each other for fifty plus years.
Thank you, Larry, for Facebooking me.

1960's Barber Shop in Chicago's Northwest Side

Issues of *Playboy*
before Hefner patched centerfolds
with pubic hair strew the coffee table.
Italian American men,
first born generation in the U.S.
leaf through the magazines.
Dense bushes block their ears.
Gray threads hang from noses.

Mario waves a clipper
buzzing near a client's jugular
who says, *last night*
a waiter was pissed with his tip.
Mario shouts, *You fucken stiffed the guy.*

Each waiting man gets his name call
tosses a publication onto the table
sits into a chair Mario pumps to a height
where without bending
he trims above the ears,
spreads warm shaving cream
on backs of necks,
before he scrapes with a blade.
Manly spices spew the air.

Before Mario lowers chairs
his middle finger
slides through the loop
of a pointed scissor's handle.
His hairy knuckled right hand
attached to a fury arm
sticks steel blades
in each patron's nostril
who pays, tips
the barber in cash.

From Play to Write

We take a break from lessons
in the yard of a Chicago public school.
I accept my turn to get chase
tackle. On my back, eyes squint sun.
The pack yanks button-down shirt
along with the undershirt out of my pants.
Slap belly pink. I join them
initiate the next inductee.
We kick rubber balls in the playground
throw them at or below classmates' chests
as instructed in gym's dodgeball games.
Endorphin driven
we learn tolerance
develop foes, friends,
in free play

like what poets do with words.
They put verbs before nouns
break lines
in middle of sentences
invent slant rhymes
fool readers to believe
no one questioned
"rage" "humanity"
since beginning of language.

Poets feel like God.

Particles at the Edge of Life

a virus 30,000 years old still ticking in plant tissue,
discovered deep in melting permafrost - Livescience.com

unlike deer who rut in autumn
sexual urges don't rage in viruses
they have no
genetic spiral staircases
unable to divide in half
organelles aren't present
like mitochondria
cells' powerhouses
makes no difference
they have no need for food
to extract energy

Thanks to Cadence Turner who tries to keep my syntax grounded, Kathy Negaard, Austin Walsh, Naples Writers Group, Quint Cities Poets, Midwest Writing Center, Steve Semken.

In memory of Mari Messer, Roald Tweet,
Dick Stahl, Max Molleston

Credits:

Used, "Put Aside Faint rubbing sound"—https://woodclinched.com/2010/09/16/listen-to-your-penci/

Roaming Souls Who Do Not have a Passage Ritual—https://english-kyoto-seas.org/wp-content/uploads/010101.pdf "Suffering Beings Who Roam" and "lingering ghost" came from this article Caring for the Dead Ritually in Cambodia by John Clifford Holt

Survivor Prays for Victims while Christ Gets Whip *What Have you Heard Is True* came from Carlyon Forche's memoir–"… tossed from helicopter into the sea. … when a body hits the water, is the same as falling into a block of stone."

Irma Kills Creation in Puerto Rico—Bees are buzzing around crazily, looking—NPR Oct 1, 2017

Particles at the Edge of Life—independent particles at the edge of life http://watershedlandcare.com.au/organisms-at-the-edge-of-life/

Safe Place—Derived from a Candance Turner poem.

This is Salvatore Marici 's fourth book of poetry. He was the 2010 Midwest Writing Center Poet-in-Resident, has judged poetry contests, placed in poetry contests, both teaches workshops and attends poetry workshops. His poetry has appeared in *Toasted Cheese, Spillway, Prairie Gold: An Anthology of the American Heartland, Of Burgers & Barrooms a Main Street Rag anthology, Poetry Quarterly* and many more. Marici served as a Peace Corps volunteer in Guatemala as a natural resources specialist and he is a civil servant retiree/ agronomist. In South West Florida he is learning to maneuver a 17-foot kayak. During the summer he grows garlic in Western Illinois.

The Ice Cube Press began publishing in 1991 to focus on how to live with the natural world and to better understand how people can best live together in the communities they share and inhabit. Using the literary arts to explore life and experiences in the heartland of the United States we have been recognized by a number of well-known writers including: Bill Bradley, Gary Snyder, Gene Logsdon, Wes Jackson, Patricia Hampl, Greg Brown, Jim Harrison, Annie Dillard, Ken Burns, Roz Chast, Jane Hamilton, Daniel Menaker, Kathleen Norris, Janisse Ray, Craig Lesley, Alison Deming, Harriet Lerner, Richard Lynn Stegner, Richard Rhodes, Michael Pollan, David Abram, David Orr, and Barry Lopez. We've published a number of well-known authors including: Mary Swander, Jim Heynen, Mary Pipher, Bill Holm, Connie Mutel, John T. Price, Carol Bly, Marvin Bell, Debra Marquart, Ted Kooser, Stephanie Mills, Bill McKibben, Craig Lesley, Elizabeth McCracken, Derrick Jensen, Dean Bakopoulos, Rick Bass, Linda Hogan, Pam Houston, and Paul Gruchow. Check out Ice Cube Press books on our web site, join our email list, Facebook group, or follow us on Twitter. Visit booksellers, museum shops, or any place you can find good books and support our truly honest to goodness independent publishing projects and discover why we continue striving to "hear the other side."

Ice Cube Press, LLC (Est. 1991)
North Liberty, Iowa, Midwest, USA
Resting above the Silurian and Jordan aquifers
steve@icecubepress.com
Check us out on twitter and facebook
www.icecubepress.com

Celebrating Thirty Years of Independent Publishing

To Fenna Marie—
sly as a fox and
a coyote trickster who just happens to
be the greatest kid

"Sal Marici's *Sneezing Coyotes* is geography as poetry—from the intimate landscapes of the human body 'unshaven jungles where mucous flourishes but also "birds, flowers align' to the landscapes we share with other creatures, including pedestrians, alligators and roaming souls. From the Mississippi to the Mekong, Marici brings us to places we adore, alter, destroy, and call home. We meet his cultivated soil with calloused feet, let it dirty our sheets, and sift it with black pepper to keep coyotes away. For those of us who try to move through the world with love for it, we might do as Sal Marici does in poetry and, I suspect, in most of his waking hours: 'do not sweep / scattered fondness' from ourselves as we pass."
—Beth Roberts, author of *Like You* (Fence, 2021),
winner of the Ottoline Prize and finalist for the
2021 Heartland Booksellers Award

"*Sneezing Coyotes* by Salvatore Marici is a surprising collection that whispers one moment and shouts the next. Filled with places and objects, this collection of poems is an interesting mix of both speed and lingering that engages the reader's curiosity and poetical spirit. The line breaks control pivotal changes and entice readers to return to these poems again and again. *Sneezing Coyotes* belongs in any serious poetry collection."
—Glenn Lyvers; Masthead, Prolific Press

"'Coyotes sniff the hole's fresh-turned soil' in Salvatore Marici's *Sneezing Coyotes*, a fitting image for poems that are simultaneously reflective, illuminating, and grave. This newest collection highlights global intersections and parallels of people at their most vulnerable: at war, sick, or dying. Though collisions occur 'inside the rush to get there,' these poems give us again familiar Marici loveliness: 'birds, flowers align.'"
—Stephen Frech, author of *Into Night's Tent*

"Every line of *Sneezing Coyotes* lures the reader into a rich, earthy underworld of decay, disease, disappearances, ghosts. Barbed images bite and sink deep, a sensuous bouquet for the ear and tongue, a deep stab to the heart. Marici's dry, unblinking gaze bears homage and witness, catching readers at the brink of despair and lifting them to possibility. Laced with sweetness and horror, violence and reverence, grime and new growth, this is Marici's best collection yet—utterly unforgettable."
—Misty Urban, author of *My Day As Regan Forrester*

"*Sneezing Coyotes* leaves no aspect of life unexamined. Infused with sharp observations both personal and worldly, Marici's newest collection of poems radiate with a full range of senses and emotions while taking the reader on a geographical and spiritual journey spanning space and time. It's through this journey Marici helps us see his array of 'networks of living systems/grown from the dead in soil,' and that death is a way of life not to be feared, but embraced."
—Kali White VanBaale, author of *The Monsters We Make* and *The Good Divide*

"Unpretentious, accessible poems that have the capacity to make you smile with recognition or alternately to weep from the longing, loss, and human want that is our common experience, no matter where in the world we live or travel."
—Carolyn Martin, Host, Talking Art, WVIK-NPR

"*Sneezing Coyotes* captures another leg of Salvatore Marici's creative journey, expanding our understanding and appreciation for viewing the world through this poet's special lens. Marici's boundless curiosity couples with his unique interpretative process to deliver a new collection of lyric gems. He weaves a connective thread through each poem, linking the surreal with the earthly, romance to science, pigs to rats and, of course, coyotes. Consuming his poems is like mind-feasting from a Whitman's Sampler box."
—John Busbee for The Culture Buzz, Des Moines, Iowa